Sarah Morgan Bryan Piatt

Child's-World Ballads

Three little emigrants, a romance of Cork Harbor, etc.

Sarah Morgan Bryan Piatt

Child's-World Ballads
Three little emigrants, a romance of Cork Harbor, etc.

ISBN/EAN: 9783744797054

Printed in Europe, USA, Canada, Australia, Japan

Cover: Foto ©Thomas Meinert / pixelio.de

More available books at **www.hansebooks.com**

CHILD'S-WORLD BALLADS

— ✠ —

Three Little Emigrants

A ROMANCE OF CORK HARBOUR, 1884

ETC.

BY

SARAH M. B. PIATT

AUTHOR OF 'A VOYAGE TO THE FORTUNATE ISLES,' ETC.

CINCINNATI

ROBERT CLARKE AND CO.

1887

CONTENTS

THREE LITTLE EMIGRANTS.

THREE LITTLE EMIGRANTS:

A ROMANCE OF CORK HARBOUR, 1884.

THE soldier's coat was English-red,
  And Irish-red was Katy's cheek:
"But he's a handsome boy," she said,
  "And it's to-night he means to speak.

"Who's English-born is not to blame
  For that! (He *would* become the green.)
Sure, but it is a burning shame
  To think he *will* stand by the Queen.

"He and Sir Garnet, side-by-side,
  Fought beautifully, though, out there,—
Faith! he's a splendid scar to hide
  With all that elegant black hair!"

9

So Katy set her cap—as clean
　As snow, pink ribbons, snares of lace—
And waited by the hedge unseen.
　(Now Katy, you will lose your place!)

At last the moon peeped, with a smile,
　Into a face that she had met
Among the palm-leaves by the Nile—
　A face the moon could not forget.

Upon the scarlet breast she spied
　The usual medal—there to tell
How bravely those dark Arabs died ?
　But Katy heard—the nursery-bell.

"Sure, that's the mistress.　She's come down
　To be a-meddling," Katy said ;
"And it's herself would say the town
　By this time ought to be in bed !"

"Where are the children, Katy ?"　"Sure,
　It is myself that ought to know !
The air to-night, ma'am, was so pure
　I stole outside a bit, and so——"

·· Where are the children ? "   " It 's asleep
    They ought to be !   Wait, ma'am, I say.
I 've been a-thinking.—Could I keep
    The things I couldn't see away ?

" Sure it 's the fairies !   They have got
    The children !   It 's their way, it is.
Faith, it 's the priest could read you what
    They 're up to, in that book of his ! "

. . . There lay the little, lonely beds.
    Above them bent a whiter face.
What hollows those three precious heads
    Had left cold in the pillow-lace !

Then, in an instant, what a flight
    There was of drowsy dreams close by !
What whispers to the pitiless night,
    And to the strangling river nigh !

Shadows with lanterns walked without.
    (One almost heard the fall of tears.)
Within—within, I do not doubt,
    The night was as a thousand years.

Scarce since that wailing midnight when
  This quaint old rebel city heard
The muffled march of Cromwell's men
  Was it so passionately stirred.·

Down that black alley, where the face
  Of Edmund Spenser peers sometimes,
Through rags and want, to see the place
  Where once a courtier writ his rhymes ;

Through Shandon's shadow, where the earth
  Lies lightly on his happy head
Who set its bells to ringing mirth,
  The trouble, like an arrow, sped.

Even the Red Abbey's buried chime
  (Made of old silver and the best)
Half-lost in legend, deep in time,
  Longed to be ringing with the rest !

. . . Meanwhile, where *were* the children ?   They
  Had heard a whistle at the gate :
" That's Katy's sweetheart.   She's away.
  Now we can go.   It isn't late.

"Make haste, or she will catch us!" So,
　Without the nurse, somehow, they dressed
And started. Whither? Did they know?
　They started—to the mighty West!

Under the stars and hand-in-hand,
　Held by another Hand, they went
Through the dim hours, as they had planned,
　To seek—another continent.

Ah me, what scent of sandal-wood,
　What glory of Atlantic gold,
Had lured them, faintly understood?
　What tales a bird of the air had told!

The charméd swans that haunt the Lee,
　A trifle fluttered, curious quite,
Sailed from their stately sleep to see
　These pretty people of the night.

Meanwhile those blue eyes saw, no doubt,
　Some wonder-sights that pleased them well:
Strange starlight creatures glimmered out
　From wayside bloom and wayside shell.

From level strongholds banners flew,
  Yellow or purple. (Only flowers,
You say?)   And one low trumpet blew
  (*Was* it the wind, indeed?) for hours.

At Irish Tivoli they feared
  To pass the evergreen's chill glooms—
For lo! a knight with sharpened beard
  Nodded Elizabethan plumes![1]

He broke a leaf or two from trees
  He planted ghostly years ago,
And hid them in his breast.—"You'll please
  Tell us the way, sir, if you know."

"I knew, my pretty folk," he said,
  "God speed you!"   Oh! his eyes were sad
And still.   And what a gracious head
  For any man to lose, he had!

They journeyed till they met the light.
  Never before was dawn so fair.
When Monkstown Castle stole in sight,
  The sunrise birds were singing there.

[1] Sir Walter Raleigh is said to have once resided at Tivoli, Cork.

Milkmen and market-women, gay
  With primrose-gold, stared blankly out
At these wee wonders of the way,
  From donkey-carts, with smile and shout.

On Queenstown Beach, a sleepy maid
  Muttered : "A pretty time to ring !"
At last she shivered, half afraid,
  Into the hall : "Sure, such a thing,"

She cried, "was never heard of yet !"
  There at the door they stood, all three
(Seven, five, and two their years) as wet
  With dew as night-drenched buds would be.

"We want some bread-and-butter, though,
  And strawberry jam and tea and cake,
If you have any.   You 're too slow !—
  We 're tired, we 've been all night awake."

Ah ! lovely sash and nun-wrought lace,
  And fairy boots of pink and blue,
How did you come to such disgrace ?—
  Whatever will your mother do ?

Far off as heaven the enchanted mast
  Was lingering on the island sky ;
The empty seas lay veiled and vast,
  The *Shamrock* [1] gave the cruel cry.

" We have to stay here now, that 's all ! "
  The boy sobbed, and he hid his face ;
" The tender 's gone.   I tried to call
  The Captain.   It 's a splendid place !—

" America, that 's what I mean.
  It *is* a splendid place.   Why not ?
Indians and bears and snakes !—I 've seen
  The pictures. . . . *But the ship forgot !* "

Then through his great still tears and vain,
  The baby hero choked his sighs. . . .
Did the grey Admiral from Spain
  Look Westward with such longing eyes ?

[1] The name of a tender.

THE CHILD MOZART AND ST. JOHN OF BOHEMIA.

B

THE CHILD MOZART AND ST. JOHN OF BOHEMIA.

THE two stood in a faëry place
 On some Bohemian hill.
The boy seemed not of our own race,
 He was so slight and still;

A lovely alien, who had strayed
 When some strange star went by,
Out of its shining ways, and stayed
 On earth, he knew not why.

Bare-headed, on that lonesome height,
 Where yet the dew was cold,
He took, as by some gracious right,
 The sun's salute of gold;

With lambs, above the world of men,
　There in the world of birds,
So looked the young Apollo, when
　He—quite forgot the herds.

Perhaps it was the winds and bees,
　Perhaps his sweet ears rung
With snatches of the melodies
　The morning stars had sung.

Yet this fair little foreign guest,
　Born somewhere in the sky,
Knew—(if the truth must be confest)
　The boy knew how to cry.

" Look, sister, look," he sadly said,
　While great tears gathered slow,
" There is no butter on my bread."
　She answered him : " I know.

" We are so poor, and that is why."
　" Well, what do people do
When they are poor ? "　" Sometimes they cry."
　(Their mother did, she knew.)

" But don't they pray, too, sometimes ? "   " Yes."
" Then, good St. John, I say
My mother needs a prettier dress ;—
    Please send one right away."

(St. John, hurled from a parapet
    At some wild Emperor's frown :
Five stars brood on the Moldau yet,
    Five stars that saw him drown.)

" We want a new piano, too ;
    Our old one used to play,
But it forgets its music.   You
    Are kind to all who pray ?

" And there's the butter, too.   But see,—
    Why, here he is ! "   And then
Came laughing from behind a tree
    The handsomest of men,

Clothed in dark forest-green, his head
    High as an oak's need be,
And shadowed by a plume.   He said :
    " Come, little ones, with me. "

And so the children's saint, the blest,
  The beautiful St. John,
Walked with them—(rather oddly drest
  You think.   Of this anon).

That day a sudden dinner, such
  As they had never seen,
Came to their table.   And how much
  They thanked the saint in green !

Bright as an autumn-leaf in bloom
  Their mother moved, and yet
That night—the absence in her room
  Made cheek and pillow wet.

That night the old piano, too,
  Grieved like a living thing,—
For the blonde boy, right well it knew,
  Had vanished with the King.

(The King, I said, but, on my word,
  It's quite another thing,—
Somewhere in history I have heard
  The Queen was then the King.[1])

[1] *"Long live our King—Maria Theresa !"*

Into a place of shining state
    The child-musician went,
In violet velvet, to await
    Court-kiss and compliment.

. . . And lo, a palace maiden bright,
    A vision to admire,
A creature made of rose and white
    And gold, in brave attire !

The boy raised his flower-face as she
    Passed him with slow regret :
" I say, and will you marry me,
    Miss Marie Antoinette ? "

" I dare not ; what would mother say ?—
    I mean the Empress, child, "
The enchanted princess answered. They
    Who listened stared and smiled.

She tossed her shining head a bit,
    With one bright backward glance ;
And Wolfgang Mozart wept when it
    Gilded the axe of France.

THE WATCH OF A SWAN.

25

THE WATCH OF A SWAN.

I READ somewhere that a swan, snow-white,
  In the sun all day, in the moon all night,
Alone by a little grave would sit
  Waiting, and watching it.

Up out of the lake her mate would rise,
And call her down with his piteous cries
Into the waters still and dim ;—
  With cries she would answer him.

Hardly a shadow would she let pass
Over the baby's cover of grass ;
Only the wind might dare to stir
  The lily that watched with her.

Do I think that the swan was an angel? Oh,
I think it was only a swan, you know,
That for some sweet reason, wingèd and wild,
  Had the love of a bird for a child.

A TRIUMPH OF TRAVEL.

29

A TRIUMPH OF TRAVEL.

AT EDINBURGH.

THERE rose the tragic palace towers
 Against the moon. (The tale was true!)
The Prince's Gardens faint with flowers
 And still with statue-spectres grew.

There, on its rock, the Castle lay,
 An awful shadow-shape forlorn,
Among the night-lamps, and, by day—
 The place where James the First was born.

There, for the Covenanters' sake,
 One haunts the grasses of Grey Friars ;
There grim John Knox had loved to shake
 His right hand full of ghostly fires.

There, changed to marble, Walter Scott
    Received the world. And Burns of Ayr,
With all his loves and debts forgot,
    A bronze immortal met you there.

No whit the seven-years' stranger cared ;
    As under gables high and still
Through immemorial dust he fared,
    He spoke his heart out with a will :

" I 'm tired of Holyrood, that 's what !
    And all the other things," he said ;
" There 's nothing in it ! She is not ;—
    I mean Queen Mary. She is dead.

" I 'm glad I did just one thing there."
    (In vain they showed him " Rizzio's bluid.")
" I put my hand on every chair
    That said ' Don't Touch ' at Holyrood ! "

THE COMING OUT OF HER DOLL.

C

THE COMING OUT OF HER DOLL.

YOUNG GIRL-GRADUATE TO HER MOTHER.

" NOW I begin to think it 's time that Rose
    Should wear a train. She 's a young lady now.
You really cannot guess how much she knows.
    (She 's read some charming novels, anyhow.)

" How sweet she 'd look in a Commencement dress,
    White satin and illusion, and some pearls.
Her gloves must have six buttons, and—I guess
    She 'd get more flowers than all the other girls.

" I fancy she should have some company.
    (Papa, he always comes home late and tired.)
And if she only had—some one, you see,
    To take her out, she would be much admired.

" Oh, you forget.   You brought her home to me
    Once on my birthday, years and years ago.
She could not be a baby yet, you see ;—
    Why, then I was a child myself, you know !"

THE LITTLE COWHERD.

THE LITTLE COWHERD.

" COME, look at her, and you will love her.
    Go, lead her now through pleasant places,
And teach her that our New-World's clover
    Is sweet as Jersey Island daisies.

" Yes, you may do a little playing
    Close to the gate, my pretty warder;
But, meanwhile, keep your cow from straying
    Across the elfin people's border."

So to the boy his mother jested
    About his light task, lightly heeding,
While in the flowering grass he rested
    The magic book that he was reading.

At sundown for the cow's returning
   The milkmaid waited long, I 'm thinking.
Hours later, by the moon's weird burning,
   Did fairy-folk have cream for drinking ?

. . . What of the boy ? By hill and hollow,
   Through bloom and brier, till twilight ended,
His book had charmed him on to follow
   The cow—the one that Cadmus tended !

A NEW KNIGHT.

41

A NEW KNIGHT.

TO A SCHOOLBOY.

HERE you sit with a picture-book,
    And stare at a knight with his armour on,
While the bird that waited for you to look
    At his scarlet coat is surely gone.
He sings too low and he sings too near ?—
It is Roland's horn you would like to hear ?

Why, the horn of Roland was only blown
    Because there was something wrong, you know,
When the world was dark. But the world has
       grown
    A trifle brighter since then, and so
We are looking around for some new knight
Whose horn shall tell us of something right.

You like the one in the picture best ?
　　Oh, he *does* look well in his plume and steel ;
But only fancy if you were dressed
　　In that odd fashion, how you would feel—
Riding along, while the boys looked through
The schoolroom windows and laughed at you !

You would storm some fortress?—You never will;
　　You sleep and you dream too much for that.
Take care lest the boy below the hill,
　　With the one wild rose in his torn straw hat,
Who climbs the rocks, while they 're dim with
　　　　dew,
To bring you milk, make his squire of you !

THE OLD KING'S ATONEMENT.

THE OLD KING'S ATONEMENT.

TOLD TO A BOY ON CHRISTMAS EVE.

THIS is the story that a dead man writ—
 Five hundred years ago it must be, quite ;
Worlds full of children listened once to it,
 Who do not ask for stories now at night.

Worlds full of children, who have followed him,
 The King they learned to love and to forgive,
About whose feet the North-snows once lay dim,
 To the sweet land where he has gone to live.

He was a boy whose purple cap could show
 As true a peacock's-plume as ever fanned
Bright royal hair, but in the gracious glow
 Of his fair head strange things, it seems, were
  planned :

"To be a prince is well enough," thought he,
  "But then would it not be a braver thing
To be—my father, only young! To be,"
  He whispered, oh, so low—"to be the King!—

"My father, who may live for years and years.
  And I meanwhile?—Prince Henry to the last!
Sin, by God's grace, may be washed out with tears,
  And some day I'll have time to pray and fast."

He blew a blast that wailed from field to field;
  Then, with his sword's point hurled his father
    down,
And bared his own dark forehead, and revealed
  Thereon the sudden lightning of the crown.

But soon that fire of jewels round his head
  Burned to his heart. He sat forlorn with grief:
"We'll send across the mountains there," he said,
  "To our great Priest in Italy for relief."

His Holiness sat thinking in his town
  Of Rome five minutes, or, it may be, more;
His scarlet Cardinals pulled their brave hats down,
  And thought as Cardinals never thought before.

"Tell him," the reverend Father said, "to build
   Strong churches, and give freely of his gold
To our poor brothers." So his realm was filled
   With monks and abbeys. But—shall truth be
      told ?—

His father's shadow would not let him be,—
   Till, one fine night, out of the pleasant skies,
Mary looked down, remembering that he
   Was once a child, with sweet half-human eyes :

"He shall be glad again, for he shall make
   The little ones glad in memory of my Son,"
She said. Her aureole flashed the King awake ;
   He thought, "Let my Lord's Mother's will be done."

So from his head the cruel crown he shook,
   And from his breast the ermine cloak he tore,
And, wrapped in serge, his lonesome way he took
   In the weird night from dreaming door to door.

A very Saint of Christmas in the moon,
   Followed by glimmering evergreens and toys,
The old King looked. And did they wake too soon,
   Those blonde-haired, blue-eyed, far-back girls and
      boys ?

I only know that still the peasants say,
　　In his far country, that a strange King walks
All night before the Lord Christ's glad birthday,
　　And leaves no track—a King who never talks!

And sometimes children, stealing from their bed,
　　To look if the slow morning yet be near,
Have seen his sweeping beard and hooded head,
　　And grey, still smile, with never any fear.

They know the dawn will light the loveliest things,
　　Left in the silence by their silent friend.
They know the strange King is the best of kings,
　　And mean to love him till the world shall end.

COMFORT THROUGH A WINDOW.

COMFORT THROUGH A WINDOW.

(CHILD WITHIN TO TRAMP WITHOUT.)

IT'S not so nice here as it looks,
　　With china that keeps breaking so,
And five of Mr. Tennyson's books
　　Too fine to look in—is it, though?

If you just had to sit here (Well!)
　　In satin chairs too blue to touch,
And look at flowers too sweet to smell,
　　In vases—would you like it much?

If you see any flowers, they grow,
　　And you can find them in the sun.
These are the ones we buy, you know,
　　In winter-time—when there are none!

53

Then you can sit on rocks, you see,
   And walk about in water, too—
Because you have no shoes! Dear me!
   How many things they let you do!

Then you can sleep out in the shade
   All day, I guess, and all night too,
Because—you know, you're not afraid
   Of other fellows just like you!

You have no house like this, you know,
   (Where mamma's cross, and ladies call)—
You have the world to live in, though,
   And that's the prettiest place of all!

FRED'S MOTHER.

MASTER HARRY'S COMMENT.

" FRED says his mother cannot tell
  One-half the things he asks her. Well !

"She doesn't even know how far
It is straight to that nearest star.

"She only knows the Golden Rule.
—I wonder where she went to school ! "

EDINBURGH UNIVERSITY PRESS:

T. AND A. CONSTABLE, PRINTERS TO HER MAJESTY.

MRS. PIATT'S SELECT POEMS.

A VOYAGE TO THE FORTUNATE ISLES, AND OTHER POEMS.

By Sarah M. B. Piatt.

Small Crown 8vo, Cloth, gilt top, 5s.

Published in the United States by HOUGHTON, MIFFLIN & Co., Boston and New York, Price $1.50.

Extracts from British Critical Opinions.

The Academy, December 5, 1885.

'The author of these poems and her work are well known on the other side of the Atlantic, and two tiny volumes of verse have recently introduced her very favourably to English readers. The present book contains a rich and excellently selected gathering from Mrs. Piatt's various works, issued in America, and it will, undoubtedly, win a warm welcome from the lovers of poetry among us, and extend the radius of her influence and reputation. Mrs. Piatt's verses are characterised by a distinct and pleasing originality. . . . Nothing more unfailingly distinguishes her poems than the solid kernel of fresh, original thought and feeling in each of them—thought and feeling which are expressed with careful and conscientious artistry. . . . Not a few of the most delicate and successful pieces of the book are to be found in the section titled, "In Company with Children." Here the womanly nature of the poet has full scope. . . . The temptation to quote further from this charming volume is almost irresistible, but we must leave the reader to discover the rest of its dainty and pathetic things for himself. The book entitles its author to a very honourable place in the roll of women poets of our century.'

The St. James's Gazette, November 21, 1885.

'We find that Mrs. Piatt's Muse is the Muse of the American Girl. . . . And we confess, for our own part, that the more completely she is the Muse of the American Girl the better we like her. There is real originality in such pieces as "If I were a Queen," "Caprice at Home," and "After the Quarrel." The reflection on Cleopatra—

> "No coward of my conqueror's race
> Should offer me his blood, I know,
>   If I were a Queen—"

is delightfully in the spirit of free Transatlantic criticism. Rhythmically, too, Mrs. Piatt is at her best in these lighter pieces. In "Caprice at Home" there is a pettishness of movement in the verse corresponding excellently to its mood. Take for example, the lines:—

> "No, I will not say good-bye,
> Not good-bye, nor anything;"

or

> "Everything I want I miss.
> Oh, a precious world is this "

Very arch, too, is "After the Quarrel," where one girl is consoling another for the loss of her lover :—

> "But he will not come?—Why, then,
> Is no other within call?
> There are men and men, and men—
> And these men are brothers all!
> Each sweet fault of his you'll find
> Just as sweet in all his kind."

There is so much room in our literature for verse which is playful without being exactly humorous, that it is to be hoped Mrs. Piatt will pursue further a vein in which she is so eminently successful. We have no wish, however, to disparage the more serious efforts of this pleasing and unpretentious writer. Like Miss Ingelow and other disciples of the great but unequal poetess of "Casa Guidi Windows," Mrs. Piatt's mood alternates between a fantastic regret and a heart-broken idealism. She bewails mystically the dead infancies of her growing children, and has dreams about them in a glorified perfection. All this is well summed up in the narrative poem from which the volume takes its title—the poem which tries to force on us the conclusion that

> "We leave the Fortunate Isles behind,
> The Fortunate Isles to find;"

and abounds in vaguely suggestive imagery, as of the butterflies

> "That glitter, homesick for the form
> And lost sleep of the worm."

'In "Two Veils" and "Her Cross and Mine," Mrs. Piatt has touched skilfully on the contrast between the world's perils and the safe shelter of the convent. "The Altar at Athens" is a rather striking presentation of the enigma of contending creeds. "The Gift of Empty Hands" and "Everything" are fables of deft invention if trite morality. The first stanza of "To-day" is worth quotation for its easy rendering of a plaintive mood :—

> "Ah, real thing of bloom and breath,
> I cannot love you while you stay.
> Put on the dim, still charm of death,
> Fade to a phantom, float away,
> And let me call you Yesterday!"

"Asking for Tears" has something of the accent of "Sonnets from the Portuguese." In the more dramatic pieces, like "The Palace-Burner," "There was a Rose," and "A Wall Between," these abrupt artifices are less inappropriate. "A Wall Between," which presents in some nine pages the scene of a husband coming in priest's disguise to the death-bed of his neglected wife, seems to be admirably adapted for recitation. The writer preserves here, as always, both delicacy and taste. The piece is a good one. But we recur to our preference of Mrs. Piatt as the lyrist of whim, the Muse of the American Girl.'

The Irish Monthly, July 1886.

'This woman-poet's poems come to us with a New World freshness and fragrance, superadded to the sweetness and tenderness, which are among the things that never grow old. Some of the poems, in their largeness and freedom, their boldness in seizing, and crying aloud the vague doubts and marvellings which have wearied and pained us all at times, not the less that we have scarcely dared to look them in the face, read like a revelation—a revelation of one's own heart, of a woman's heart. The book is essentially a woman's book, though, in its breadth of treatment, it has often a masculine quality of strength,—it is the book of a woman who is also a wife, and the mother of children, and in the noble attributes of a developed womanliness, the poetry of it must rank almost with the highest. . . . Three women's names suggest themselves to the present writer, as those of distinct and individual singers in our own day—Christina Rossetti, Jean Ingelow, and Alice Meynell, whose one exquisite volume " Preludes," is an embodiment of the purest poetry; and to those three names Sarah Piatt's may now be added as a fourth, for her marked originality and freshness are wonderful, in an age more than a score of hundred years after Solomon bewailed the staleness of all things under the sun. The tenderness, the purity of the book, is beyond all praise ; and the curious current and undertone of pathos running through the highest strain—a sadness entirely natural, and not at all a literary quality, as so much present-day sadness seems to be—gives the work an ennobling gravity. From this true, sweet poet one wishes to quote largely, feeling that the poems speak best for their own excellence ; but where all is perfect, there is a difficulty in selection. . . . The poem which gives the first book its name is wise and beautiful, and " A Wall Between " contains some of the best things the poet has given us. . . . It has some wonderful passages. . . . Perhaps the short poems are the most perfect, and the style at its best is limpidly clear. . . . Any notice of this book would be incomplete, however abundant its citations, if it failed to quote from the poems concerning children, which, perhaps, more than any other feature, set the book apart from any other book we have ever read. Its insight into child-life, the *naïveté* of a child's thoughts, here so accurately rendered, will make the book especially lovable to grown lovers of children, though here, perhaps, it stops short ; it will hardly reach the children themselves, as Hans Andersen, the prophet of children, does ; but rather like Mr. R. L. Stevenson's "Child's Garden of Verses," it will make the grown reader sigh and wonder at the vivid reflection from his own childhood. . . . And now, with little further quotation, we must leave this lovely and lovable book, in which is contained the cream's cream, the best perfection of the author's work. Let all who love poetry, and happily they are many, read the book for themselves, and know the delight we have felt in its reading. For the delicate grace of the book, the yearning sadness which fills one with a pain better than pleasure, for this laying open of a beautiful heart, we are deeply thankful. . . . We have tried to say little and quote much, because we felt how poorly we could say all the book makes us feel—one could say it, perhaps, better in verse than in prose, where enthusiasm finds hardly a fitting vehicle of expression. Only we thank tne writer for the gift she has given us and the world—a gift as perfect and spontaneous as the song of a blackbird, as passionate and innocent as the heart of a rose.'

The Westminster Review, July 1886.

'Many ot Mrs. Piatt's verses are concerned with the sayings and doings of children. We are ot those who hold that both the pathos and the humour of the nursery should be reserved for home consumption, but for those who think otherwise with regard to the "Kingdom of Heavenites," as Coleridge called babies, we can safely recommend Mrs. Piatt. Among the more striking poems in this volume are "A Voyage to the Fortunate Isles," "The Longest Death-Watch," and "Twelve Hours Apart." We select for quotation a double quatrain, entitled "Broken Promise."'

Merry England (Review of Professor Robertson's "Children of the Poets"), March 1887.

'Mrs. Piatt is an American writer not yet known to many in England, though quickly recognised by a few. She never writes without thoughts, and her thoughts, though not always concentrated, are always distinct, and with distinctness they have a rare distinction. This beauty of thought will always be, in spite of the perfect things that have been done in mere form, the supreme merit of poetry and of all literature. But as regards utterance also Mrs. Piatt does exquisitely, having a restraint of tone, a moderation of emphasis, of length, which show firm and careful art; and a quite simple vocabulary. One of her loveliest poems is this in the "Children of the Poets." It is headed "Last Words," and is spoken over a little bed at night.'

The Pictorial World, June 3, 1886.

'Mrs. Piatt is an American woman of genius, and the pensive tone and sweet natural music which distinguish her verse have produced, in "A Voyage to the Fortunate Isles," etc., poems of a delicate beauty, not easy to equal, much less surpass, on either side of the Atlantic. The thought, the expression of these poems are alike purely womanly. Mrs. Piatt studies no model, and takes no pattern for her work; she simply expresses herself; hence her verse is just the transparent mantle of her individuality. The natural refinement, the ready sympathy, the tender sentiment, the quiet grace of a thoroughly womanly woman reveal themselves quite unconsciously in every poem; and the musical quality of the verse increases the impression that the reader is listening to the heart-utterances of one of the Imogens or Mirandas to be met with now seldom outside the radiant land where Shakespeare's imagination reigns supreme. . . . The poems "In Company with Children" contain some of the most distinctive and original of Mrs. Piatt's work. She has especial power of entering into the child life, and she is not afraid to let the children speak in her verse as they speak in life. "My Babes in the Wood," "Playing Beggars," "The Little Boy I Dreamed About," "The Baby's Brother," are a few of many poems which occupy in the realm of verse a quiet corner entirely their own. . . . Mrs. Piatt will, we doubt not, as her poems become known to English readers, become popular, or, we should rather say, dear to a wide circle mainly composed of members of her own sex, for she supplies the adequate expression for women whose hearts are tender and true like her own.'

The Dublin Evening Mail, April 7, 1886.

'If Mrs. Piatt's "Irish Garland" contains poetry like that in the volume before us, it ought to be placed forthwith in the best hundred Irish books. . . . Originality, simplicity, tenderness, and a profoundly pathetic sense of things are the notes of Mrs. Piatt's muse. In many passages she reminds us of Mrs. Barrett Browning, but she is more lyrical, less rhetorical . . . America may be proud of Mrs. Piatt, and we believe is so.'

The Literary World, January 1, 1886.

'One of the finest poems in the book is "The Brother's Hand," founded upon a story of the American Civil War. There is a good deal of power, passion, and pathos in it. It is the longest poem in the book, and is marked by much true feeling and great narrative skill."

London Figaro, February 20, 1886.

'It was high time, though, that acquaintance was made with so charming a writer, who, while reminding us of our Jean Ingelow and Adelaide Proctor, has indubitable originality—and originality, too, of a very rare kind—of her own. . . . In so short a notice it is, indeed, difficult to even name the beauties of her characteristic muse. Allusion must be made, however, to her wonderful, and, as it would seem, intuitive power of analysing child-nature. Many of her poems deal with children, and her happiest and most winsome touches are to be found in them. Mrs. Piatt possesses genuine imagination, and, moreover, that dramatic instinct which helps so greatly to make a poem intense and vivid. . . . But to multiply quotations is impossible, and we must be content with giving the two stanzas with which Mrs. Piatt concludes this delightful volume. She says :—

"Sweet World, if you will hear me now :
I may not own a sounding Lyre
And wear my name upon my brow
Like some great jewel quick with fire.

But let me, singing, sit apart,
In tender quiet with a few,
And keep my fame upon my heart,
A little blush-rose wet with dew."

There is the melody of real poetry here.'

The Saturday Review, March 13, 1886.

'Of all the concourse of singers, ungallantly described in their own land as "female poets," Mrs. Piatt is the most racy and, in a word, the most American. Mr. Stedman finds her charming "at her best," and Miss Preston most judiciously commends her delightful poems of children. Mr. Howells praises her that "she has not written like a man," and the Boston *Repository* takes Mr. Howells to task for praising "the feminine quality" of Mrs. Piatt's muse. For our part, we are at issue with the *Repository* lady (as we must assume the critic to be), and are touched with the felicity of Mr. Howells' remarks. The new selection of Mrs. Piatt's poems should be most welcome to all who seek in American poetry something more than a pale reflex of the British commodity. In the goodly company of poetesses, all dight in their singing robes, Mrs. Piatt's part is that of the *ingénue*. Her poems, with all their whim and inconstancy of mood, are charmingly sincere, artless, piquant, and full of quaint surprise. Her pathos is not less individual, though we like her best in her "Dramatic Persons and Moods," in such poems as "Sometime," "If I were a Queen," "After the Quarrel," "Enchanted," and the like. The reflections of the speaker in the second poem in rejecting the example of all historic queens are exquisitely girl-like and natural, even to the rejection of Cleopatra :—

"Then she of Egypt—with the asp
To drain my deadly beauty dry?—
To see my Roman lover clasp
His sword with surer love, and die

Closer to it than me ? Not so.
No desert-snake with nursing grace
Should draw my fierce heart's fiercest glow ;
No coward of my conqueror's race
Should offer me his blood, I know—
If I were a Queen."

'Very startling is the quaint epigram in the first stanza of "Marble or Dust?":—

"A child, beside a statue, said to me,
With pretty wisdom very sadly just,
'That man is Mr. Lincoln, Mama. He
Was made of marble ; we are made of dust.'"

The Nation (Dublin), December 5, 1885.

'The titular poem in Mrs. Piatt's collection, "A Voyage to the Fortunate Isles," is an allegory whose lesson is, that in seeking for distant happiness we miss that which is within our grasp. The thought is an old one that has furnished food for meditation to the poet and philosopher since the earliest ages. Paradise itself was not free from these illusory ambitions. Love of change and desire of power and knowledge were what urged our first parents to their great transgression. It is no slight praise of Mrs. Piatt's poem, to say that, on a theme coeval with the world, and that in every generation has found its exponents among the greatest poets, our author has found a new and attractive figure by which to convey the old but ever necessary warning against restlessness and discontent. . . . In her description of children and their ways Mrs. Piatt could not be surpassed for accuracy and pathos. With intensified womanly fondness her whole heart goes out to them, as she watches their movements with the deep interest of her loving, sympathetic nature. . . . We would wish, did the limits of our space permit, to consider more at length these extraordinary and, with all their sadness, really beautiful poems, as they are well worthy of minute and careful study."

The Graphic, January 16, 1886.

'It is amply borne out by the present collected edition of her poems, the music and finish of which it is almost superfluous to praise. But, whilst acknowledging the author's great gifts, we cannot join in the chorus of unlimited praise which seems to be the rule in America. She has been compared to Mrs. Browning, and undoubtedly, the influence of the great English poet-woman is most apparent—one most powerful piece, "A Wall Between," is almost worthy of the author of "Bertha in the Lane." . . . The book is a striking one . . . and must not be neglected by any one who would form a just estimate of modern poetic art.'

The Scotsman, January 1, 1886.

'There is a fugitive beauty, a magical suggestiveness about her poetry.'

The Freeman's Journal, February 19, 1886.

'Her poetry is singularly pretty, tuneful and tender, and many of her pieces, especially the descriptive and narrative ones, rise to the highest level.'

KEGAN PAUL, TRENCH & CO., Publishers,
1 Paternoster Square, London.

'Quality and not quantity is what we ask for from the poet, and some of the loveliest poems in the language are also among the briefest. Here are two tiny volumes that deserve a word of praise from the critic and recognition from the public.'—London Illustrated News, June 20, 1885.

AN IRISH GARLAND. By Sarah M. B. Piatt.

Small Crown 8vo.   Cloth 3s. 6d.

Published in the United States by HOUGHTON, MIFFLIN & Co. Boston and New York, Price $1.00.

The Scotsman, December 26, 1884.

'There is a peculiar charm in the short poem entitled "In Clonmel Parish Churchyard," and another poem, "The Confession of My Neighbour," gives us one of those quick instinctive glimpses into a woman's heart which is apt to escape man's grosser vision.'

The Academy, March 21, 1885.

'This is a charming little book, and we could wish it were much longer. Rarely, indeed, has so much thought and feeling been put into verse of the secondary order with more flow and felicity of diction. . . . We can sincerely recommend Mrs. Piatt's pretty, thoughtful, and tuneful volume.'

The Graphic, July 11, 1885.

'Pathos distinguishes the best pieces, such as, "On the Pier at Queenstown," and "The Confession of My Neighbour," but there is a vein of quaint humour in places, as in a charming little childlike poem, "Comfort through a Window."'

The Saturday Review, July 11, 1885.

'Mrs. Piatt's slender volume risks overlooking by its mere slightness. It contains one poem, "The Gift of Tears," which for deep-hearted suggestiveness and concentrated pathos might have proceeded from Mrs. Browning. The kinship we claim for it is no light thing, and it is not lightly claimed.'

The Pilot (Boston, U.S.A.), April 18, 1885.

'Ought to endear her to every Irish Heart.'

THE CHILDREN OUT-OF-DOORS.

A BOOK OF VERSES. By Two in One House.

Small Crown 8vo.   Cloth, 3s. 6d.

Published in the United States by ROBERT CLARKE & CO., Cincinnati,. Price $1.25.

The Atlantic Monthly (Boston), April 1885.

'The authors of the charming book of verse called "The Children Out-of-Doors" are, of course, Mr. and Mrs. Piatt. Though their names do not appear on the title-page, their work is too characteristic to pass unrecognised.'

DAVID DOUGLAS, Publisher,

15 Castle Street, Edinburgh.

IN PRIMROSE TIME—A NEW IRISH GARLAND.

By Sarah M. B. Piatt.

Small Crown 8vo.   Cloth, gilt top, 2s. 6d.

Published in the United States by HOUGHTON, MIFFLIN & CO.,
Boston and New York, Price $1.

The Saturday Review, May 15, 1886.

'There is a fresh scent of spring and flowers about the poems.'

The Spectator, September 25, 1886.

'If we cannot justly say that Mrs. Piatt's tiny volume contains "infinite riches in a little room," we can say that her pages will give pleasure to every reader.'

The Athenæum, August 21, 1886.

'This latest volume of Mrs. Piatt's . . . has its full measure of that distinctive charm which consists in the blending of genuine pathos with that mirth which has in it something almost sadder—just as smiles under certain circumstances may be sadder than tears. . . . Here is a quaint and charming lyric, "The Awakening of the Birds," which is entirely Mrs. Piatt's own, as, indeed, is all she writes. It is not often that one has to regret the brevity of a volume of verse, but such in the present instance is the case.'

The Graphic, June 26, 1886.

'Everything that Mrs. Piatt writes must arrest attention, and these short poems, inspired by her residence in the Sister Isle, are among the most graceful and suggestive of her verses. Throughout, humour, pathos, and tender feeling are quaintly blended, and the result is most agreeable.'

The Lady, June 17, 1886.

'Mrs. Piatt's poems are always welcome, and the small volume, "In Primrose Time," contains too few of them.'

The Glasgow Herald, July 5, 1886.

'There is much that is pleasant and bright in "In Primrose Time." . . . Thoughtful readers will find more to please them in Mrs. Piatt's slim, dainty little book than in many more pretentious volumes of verse.'

The Liverpool Mercury, June 5, 1886.

'The volume must not be judged of by its size. It may be slender, but what it contains is far from being slight. Every stanza in the opening poem, from which the title of the book is taken, is quite a word-picture, while there is a peculiar freshness and sweetness about the whole. "An Irish Fairy Story," "A Portrait at Youghal," and "The Legend of Monkstown," are all equally admirable in their way; and there will be few readers, we imagine, who will not desire that each of them had been longer. There is not a poem in this book but is full of womanly instinct, and the quick, sharp insight of a woman's heart and eye. . . . Her present dainty little volume may well endear her to every warm-hearted native of Erin.'

The Freeman's Journal, June 18, 1886.

'Mrs. Piatt's little book, beautifully produced . . . adds one other to the many reasons already piled up for Ireland's love and gratitude to America and its people.'

KEGAN PAUL, TRENCH & CO., Publishers,
1 Paternoster Square, London.